Jeremy Taylor

**Poems and Verse Translations**

Jeremy Taylor

**Poems and Verse Translations**

ISBN/EAN: 9783744709347

Printed in Europe, USA, Canada, Australia, Japan

Cover: Foto ©Thomas Meinert / pixelio.de

More available books at **www.hansebooks.com**

MISCELLANIES

OF

The Fuller Worthies' Library.

THE

# POEMS

AND

## VERSE-TRANSLATIONS

OF THE

RIGHT REV. JEREMY TAYLOR, D.D.

LORD BISHOP OF DOWN, CONNOR, AND DROMORE.

FOR THE

FIRST TIME COLLECTED AND EDITED

AFTER THE AUTHOR'S OWN TEXT:

WITH

INTRODUCTION.

BY THE

REV. ALEXANDER B. GROSART.

ST. GEORGE'S, BLACKBURN, LANCASHIRE.

PRINTED FOR PRIVATE CIRCULATION.

1870.

100 COPIES ONLY.

# Contents.

# CONTENTS.

# I. Introduction.

WILLMOTT, HEBER, AND BONNEY— the order being a descending scale of worth —have written the Life in full, of JEREMY TAYLOR—and since her martyr-days, the Church of England has had few more lovely in their lives, few more intrinsically apostolic. A beautiful, modestly-heroic, pathetic, memorable Life it was: none the less Christly that it has inscribed over its academic commencement '*pauper scholaris*'—like unto the Lord's poor pair of turtle doves offered for Him.

I am not called upon to estimate our Worthy as a Theologian or Polemic. Briefly—if his thought must be pronounced beneath his eloquence, and his eloquence more resonant than illuminative, and his multifarious reading cumbersome to him as a Preacher as was Saul's armour to David—so that one yearns o'times for the simple 'sling and pebble' of a direct simple statement of "The

A                61

Way, the Truth and the Life " and would prefer
a beechen cup or homeliest ware full of " living
water " to the richest goblet surcharged with
perfumed distillations, even when the fragrance
comes from Roses of Sharon—on the other hand,
he stands supreme in English Theological literature as a pulpit-orator. " If, remarks Dr. George
Macdonald, " he had written verse equal to his
prose, he would have had a lofty place amongst
poets as well as amongst preachers."* This will
be universally conceded. As it is, what of verse-
proper he has left, deserves, if I err not, higher
recognition than it has hitherto met. I grant
there are conceits and quibbles—the smoke
rather than the flame of Fancy : but even his
conceits are rich as the gems that encrust an
Eastern nargilly. The thinking generally appears
to me more substantive and compacted than in his
prose, wide, and grand, and potent, the march of it
radiant and solemn, the music and involute rhyme
and rhythm stately, with occasional felicities alike
of idea and wording, glancing out of the Cowley-
Pindaric stanzas like the scarlet of the cactus from
its fantastic lobes of prickles. I may here con-
tinue my quotation from " Antiphon " : " They

---

* " Antiphon " p. 217.

[the Festival Hymns] bear marks, observes Dr.
Macdonald further, " of the careless impatience
of rhythm and rhyme of one who though ever
bursting into a natural trill of song, sometimes
with more rhymes apparently than he intended,
would yet rather let his thoughts pour themselves
out in that unmeasured chant, that " poetry in
solution", which is the natural speech of the
prophet orator. He is like a full river that must
flow, which rejoices in a flood, and rebels against
the constraint of mole or conduit. He exults in
utterance itself, caring little for the mode, which
however, the law of his indwelling melody guides
though never compels. Charmingly diffuse in his
prose, his verse ever sounds as if it would over-
flow the banks of its self-imposed restraints ". *
The examples chosen by the Critic are " The second
hymn for Advent ", the second " for Christmas "
and the prayers "My soul doth pant toward
Thee " and " for Charity." In the first he notes
"a little confusion of imagery ; and in others of
them . . . . . . . a little obscurity ". Of the first
prayer he remarks, " This last is quite regular,
that is, the second stanza is arranged precisely as
the first, though such will not appear to be the

---

* " Antiphon " p. 218.

case without examination : the disposition of the lines, so various in length, is confusing though not confused." Then summarily, "In these poems will be found that love of homeliness which is characteristic of all true poets. The meeting of the homely and the grand is heaven."*

The following is the original title-page of the volume in which all the Festival Hyms, save one —of which anon—first appeared, and which is our text.

The

GOLDEN GROVE

or

A MANÚALL

of

Daily Prayers and Letanies,

Fitted to the dayes of the Week.

Containing a short Summary of

What is to be { Believed,
Practised,
Desired.

---

also .

FESTIVAL HYMNS

According to the manner of

*The Ancient Church.*

---

* Antiphon, pp. 221, 222.

64

Composed for the Use of the Devout, especially
of Younger Persons; By the Author of
The Great Exemplar.

London, Printed by J. F. for R. Royston, at the
Angel in Ivie Lane, 1655. [12mo.]

A second edition appeared in 1657 with the
Author's name thus " By Jer: Taylor, D.D.
Chaplain in Ordinary to his late Majesty"—a
valiant announcement in the circumstances. The
third edition I have not succeeded in tracing : but
the 4th appeared in 1659 : and from it I take the
second Christmas Hymn, " Awake my Soul "
which was not in the 1st or 2nd edition. Curi-
ously and blameably neither Bishop Heber and
Pitman earlier, nor Eden more recently, in their
collective editions of Taylor's Works, observed
this precious addition to the " Festival Hymns,"
and hence it is not included by either.

In a long and sharp Epistle " to the pious and
devout Reader " explanation is given of the
motive and purpose of the treatise of the " Golden
Grove "—name recalling VAUGHAN—and I take
these closing references to the Hymns from it :
" Christian religion is admirable for its wisdome,
for its simplicity, and he that presents these
papers to thee, designs to teach thee as the

65

Church was taught in the early days of the Apostles. To believe the Christian Faith, and to represent plain rules of good life; to describe easie forms of prayer; to bring into your Assemblies hymnes of glorification and thanksgiving, and psalms of prayer. By these easie paths they lead Christ's little ones into the Fold of their great Bishop; and if by this way service be done to God, any ministry to the soule of a childe or an ignorant woman, it is hoped that God will accept it; and it is reward enough, if by my ministery God will bring it to pass, that any soul shall be instructed and brought into that state of good things that it shall rejoyce for ever."

Published in 1655 it is no great marvel that the " still small voice" of these Hymns and Songs for the " simple ones "—in a good tender sense— of the Church, went unheard or at least unheeded by the majority. No more a marvel that when the tempestuous season was past, listeners were found—much as after the Winter, grown men pause to catch the vernal singing of the lowliest bird. Beyond the successive editions of the " Golden Grove " and related treatises, the Hymns passed into various collections—as the Hymnologies and bibliography of Hymns shew. Thither the student will turn. JAMES MONTGOMERY called

attention in fitting words to the Hymns in his
"Christian Poet" (1825) where he quotes several
and remarks, " his verse, as might be expected is
crude, but rich in noble thoughts ". Heber fol-
lowed, by inserting in his Collection—published
posthumously in 1827—the second Hymn for
Advent and the Prayer for Charity, altered. More
recently and representing Nonconformity, the
Hymn for Advent is found in the Leeds Congrega-
tional Collection : and in the Sarum ' Hymnal '
edited by Earl Nelson and others. It appears
also in its original text in Sir Roundell Palmer's
" Book of Praise ".

I would only notice one flagrant misappropriation
viz. by SAMUEL SPEED in his " Prison Piety : or
Meditations divine and moral. Digested into
poetical heads on mixt and various subjects .

. . . by Samuel Speed, Prisoner in Ludgate,
London " (1677). Without name or marking
this unworthy scion of quaint and venerable JOHN
SPEED, has incorporated substantially the whole
of Taylor's Hymns—with such changes as take
the gipsy-form of defacing in order to conceal the
larceny. I note below the pages in " Prison-
Piety " where the several Hymns will be found :*

* Pages 102, 103 (2), 104, 110, 131, 137, 141 ¸2) 142,

and were it worth-while—which it is not—I
might go over the whole collection, and convict of
like felonies against other poets and singers of
Zion's songs, leaving nothing of any value the
lawful property of SPEED.  I had intended re-
printing " Prison-Piety ", and had spent no little
time and labour in searching out facts of the
obscure and worthless life.  But I need hardly
say that I have now no intention of reviving the
book or the memory.  I must ask pardon of the
shade of our Worthy for having momentarily
forgotten him in my quotation " of Death " in
PHINEAS FLETCHER (I., cclxxxiv—v.)  I owe
thanks to my friendly correspondent, Mr. W. T.
Brooke, London, for much help in bringing
together super-abundant proofs of the appropria-
tions, that is, misappropriations of SPEED.  I
suppose he satisfied what fragment of conscience
he had by these words in his Epistle " to the
devout "—"I have *compiled* and composed this
Manual of Meditations."

Hitherto these Hymns have been either
mangled as by Speed or modernized and otherwise
altered, as by the best editors of Taylor, *e.g.*,

143.  See examples of Speed's Readings in our notes at
close of the Hymns.

Heber and Pitman, and Eden and the Collections.
I for the first time, in later days, return to the
original text and orthography, and as already
pointed out, restore the fine Christmas hymn
"Awake my soul", so culpably overlooked by
Heber and Eden. In Notes and Illustrations a
few variations from the 1657 edition are added.

Besides the Festival Hymns in the "Golden
Grove" I have the pleasure to give Taylor's
rendering of Job's curse, *not* in the bewildering
form WILLMOTT has presented it from Playford's
"Harmonia Sacra"—as exhibited in our Note
in its place—but from "Miscellanea Sacra : or
Poems on Divine and Moral Subjects. Collected
by N. Tate, Servant to his Majesty. London :
Printed for Hen. Playford in the Temple-Change
in Fleet-street " (1696)—2nd edition, 1698. The
text of "Miscellanea Sacra" vindicates itself as
opposed to the same Publisher's "Harmonia
Sacra."

Further, it is no common satisfaction to me to
embody in this little gathering certain utterly
neglected verse-renderings of quotations from the
Classics in our illustrious prelate's works.
Throughout his numerous Writings—sermons included—Bishop Taylor is fond of working into the
web of his own thinking, the cloth-of-gold of lines

from the ancient Poets of Greece and Rome, and
later: and with reference to the Sermons more
especially, one wonders if he really delivered *ore
rotundo*, the abundant Greek and Latin that
speckle his pages. Most are left in the original.
Occasionally he renders into musical prose, also
occasionally into rhymed verse. These latter
which I designate *Aurea Grana* I have carefully
gleaned from his " Deus Justificatus " and " Discourse of the Nature and Offices of Friendship ".
I do not think that any other of his books con-
tain in text so much as one couplet more : but
below I invite attention to Lines from the Engrav-
ings of the " Great Exemplar." It is extremely
interesting to come on these additional proofs of
the poetic yearning if it may not be called " the
vision and the faculty divine". Those in
" Friendship " are extremely noticeable as having
been addressed to " the matchless Orinda "—a
lady egregiously over-lauded in her brief day.
Perhaps her (imagined) poetical gifts may have
stimulated Taylor to emulation. At any rate he
translates into verse all his quotations in the
"Discourse of Friendship". He had a sufficiently
humble estimate of his success in so far as these
minor things went : witness these words in " Deus
Justificatus, " which anticipate Dr. Macdonald's

criticism *(supra)*—" I could translate these also
[from Horace] into bad English verse as I do the
others ; but that now I am earnest for my liberty,
I will not so much as confine myself to the measures of feet ". I have given the original in each
instance, and as much of the context—the quartz
wherein the golden grains glitter—as seemed necessary for the elucidation of the translations. There
is not always closeness but there is almost invari-
ably smoothness and harmony in advance of the
Hymns, though by the nature of the quotations,
none of their largeness and opulence of thought.
I owe thanks to Eden's collective edition of the
Works for verification of some of the references :
" Deus Justificatus " in Vol. VII. pp 493—538
and " Friendship " in Vol. I. pp 69—98 : but I
reproduce the genuine orthography from the 1656
edition of the former, and that of 1657 of the
latter. I must also ask it to be kept in mind that
the prose context given, follows, as do the verse-
renderings, Taylor's own text, not Heber-Pitman
or Eden, who modernize and blunder sorrowfully.
Finally, there will be found four verse-portraits of
the four Evangelists. These are engraved under
their respective portraits in the 1657 edition of the
" Great Exemplar ", and are not included in any
of the modern collective or separate editions of

this noble book, though they were continued until
the plates were worn out. There seem to me true
poetic touches, if only touches, in some of these
Lines, and the traditional symbols of the Evangelists are well described.

So I put into the hands for the lips and hearts
of the select Readers of our Worthies, these Poems
of Bishop Jeremy Taylor, saying of him with
Wordsworth,

> " Thanks to his pure imaginative soul,
> Capacious and serene, his blameless life,
> His knowledge, wisdom, love of truth, and love
> Of human-kind."

ALEXANDER  B.  GROSART.

St. George's, Blackburn.

## II. Festival Hymns.

*"I will sing with the spirit, and I will sing with the understanding also."*

[1 Corinthians xiv. 15.  G.]

### HYMNS

CELEBRATING THE MYSTERIES AND CHIEF FESTIVALS OF THE YEAR, ACCORDING TO THE MANNER OF THE ANCIENT CHURCH: FITTED TO THE FANCY AND DEVOTION OF THE YOUNGER AND PIOUS PERSONS,

*Apt for memory, and to be joyned to their other PRAYERS.*

---

Hymns for Advent, or the weeks immediately before the Birth of our blessed Saviour.

### I.

WHEN Lord, O when shall we
　　Our dear salvation see?
　　Arise, arise,
　　Our fainting eyes
Have long'd all night; and 'twas a long one too.
Man never yet could say

He saw more then one day,
　One day of Eden's seven :
The guilty hours there blasted with the breath
　　　Of Sin and Death,
Have ever since worn a nocturnal hue.
But Thou hast given us hopes that we
At length another day shall see,
　Wherein each vile neglected place,
　Gilt with the aspect of Thy face,
Shall be like that, the porch and gate of Heaven.
　How long, dear God, how long!
　See how the nations throng :
　All humane kinde
　Knit and combin'd
Into one body, look for Thee their Head.
　Pity our multitude ;
　Lord we are vile and rude,
Headless and sensless without Thee,
Of all things but the want of Thy blest face ;
　　　　　O haste apace !
And Thy bright Self to this our body wed,
　That through the influx of Thy power,
　Each part that er'st confusion wore
　May put on order, and appear
　Spruce as the childhood of the year,
When Thou to it shalt so united be.
　　　　　　　　Amen.

The Second Hymn for Advent; or Christ's coming
to Jerusalem in Triumph.

LORD come away,
　　Why dost Thou stay?
　　Thy rode is ready; and Thy paths,
　　　　made strait,
With longing expectation, wait
The consecration of Thy beauteous feet.
Ride on triumphantly; behold we lay
Our lusts and proud wills in Thy way.
Hosanna! welcome to our hearts! Lord, here
Thou hast a temple too, and full as dear
As that of Sion, and as full of sin:
Nothing but thieves and robbers dwel therein,
Enter, and chase them forth, and cleanse the
　　　　floore;
Crucifie them, that they may never more
　　　Profane that holy place
　　Where Thou hast chose to set Thy face.
And then if our stiff tongues shall be
Mute in the praises of Thy Deity;
　　　The stones out of the Temple-wall
　　　Shall cry aloud and call
Hosanna! and Thy glorious footsteps greet.
　　　　　　　　　　　Amen.

## Hymns for Christmas-day.

### I.

**M**YSTERIOUS truth! that the self-same
should be
A Lamb, a Shepherd, and a Lion too !
Yet such was He
Whom first the shepherds knew,
When they themselves became
Sheep to the Shepherd-Lamb.
Shepherd of men and angels, Lamb of God,
Lion of Judah, by these titles keep
The wolf from Thy indangered sheep.
Bring all the world unto Thy fold,
Let Jews and Gentiles hither come
In numbers great that can't be told,
And call Thy lambs that wander, home.
Glory be to God on high,
All glories be to th'glorious Deity.

### The Second Hymn ; being a Dialogue between Three Shepherds.

**W**HERE is this blessed Babe
That hath made
All the world so full of joy
And expectation ;

That glorious Boy
That crowns each nation
With a triumphant wreath of blessedness?

Where should He be but in the throng,
                    And among
His angel-ministers, that sing
                    And take wing
Just as may echo to His voyce,
                    And rejoyce
  When wing and tongue and all
  May so procure their happiness?

But He hath other waiters now ;
                    A poor cow,
An ox and mule stand and behold,
                    And wonder,
That a stable should enfold
                    Him that can thunder.
CHORUS.   O what a gracious God have we !
  How good ? how great ? Even as our misery.


The Third Hymn : of Christ's Birth in an Inne.

HE blessed virgin travail'd without pain,
        And lodgèd in an inne ;
        A glorious star the sign,
But of a greater guest then ever came that way ;

For there He lay
That is the God of night and day,
And over all the pow'rs of heaven doth reign.
It was the time of great Augustus tax,
And then He comes
That pays all sums,
Even the whole price of lost humanity ;
And set us free
From the ungodly emperie
Of sin, and Satan, and of death.
O make our hearts, blest God, Thy lodging-place,
And in our brest
Be pleas'd to rest,
For thou lov'st temples better then an inne,
And cause that sin
May not profane the Deity within,
And sully o're the ornaments of grace.   Amen.


[The Fourth] Hymn for Christmas Day.

WAKE, my soul, and come away !
Put on thy best array;
Least if thou longer stay,
Thou lose some minitts of so blest a day.      .
Goe run,
And bid good morrow to the sun :

Welcome his safe return,
      to Capricorn;
  And that great morne
  Wherein a God was borne,
  Whose story none can tell
But He Whose every word's a miracle.
  To-day Almightiness grew weak;
The Worde itself was mute, and could not speak.
  That Jacob's star Which made the sun
  To dazle it he durst look on,
  Now mantled ore in Beth'lem's night,
  Borrowed a star to shew Him light.
    He that begirt each zone,
    To Whom both poles are one,
    Who grasp't the Zodiack in's hand
    And made it move or stand,
    Is now by nature MAN,
    By stature but a span;
  Eternitie is now grown short;
  A King is borne without a court;
  The water thirsts; the fountain's dry;
  And Life being borne, made apt to dye.
*Chorus.*  Then let our prayers emulate and vie
      With His humilitie:
  Since Hee's exil'd from skeyes
    That we might rise,—
  From low estate of men

Let's sing Him up agen!
Each man winde up's heart
To bear a part
In that angelick quire, and show
His glory high as He was low!
Let's sing t'wards men good wil and charity,
Peace upon Earth, glory to God on high
Hallelujah, Hallelujah!


3 Hymn upon St John's day.

THIS day
We sing
The friend of our eternal King:
Who in His bosome lay.
And kept the keys
Of His profound and glorious mysteries:
Which to the world dispensèd by his hand,
Made it stand
Fix'd in amazement to behold that light
Which came
From the throne of the Lamb,
To invite
Our wretched eyes—which nothing else could see
But fire, and sword, hunger and miserie—
To anticipate by their ravish'd sight
The beauty of celestial delight.

Mysterious God, regard me when I pray
And when this load of clay
Shall fall away,
O let Thy gracious hand conduct me up,
Where on the Lamb's rich viands I may sup :
And in this last Supper I
May with Thy friend in Thy sweet bosome lie
For ever in Eternity.

Allelujah.

### Upon the Day of the Holy Innocents.

MOURNFUL Iudah shreeks and cries
At the obsequies
Of their babes, that cry
More that they lose the paps, then that they die.
He that came with life to all,
Brings the babes a funeral,
To redeem from slaughter Him
Who did redeem us all from sin.
They like Himself went spotless hence,
A sacrifice to Innocence ;
Which now does ride
Trampling upon Herod's pride :
Passing from their fontinels of clay
To heaven, a milky and a bloody way.

All their tears and groans are dead
And they to rest and glory fled.
Lord, Who wert pleased so many babes should fall
Whil'st each sword hop'd that every of the all
Was the desirèd king : make us to be
In innocence like them, in glory, Thee.

Amen.

## Upon the Epiphany, and the Three Wise Men of the East coming to Worship Jesus.

A COMET dangling in the aire,
      Presag'd the ruine both of Death and
         Sin ;
   And told the wise-men of a King,
   The King of Glory, and the Sun
   Of Righteousness, Who then begun
To draw towards that blesed Hemisphere.
   They from the furthest East this new
   And unknown light pursue,
         Till they appeare
In this blest Infant-King's propitious eye ;
And pay their homage to His Royalty.
Persia might then the rising Sun adore,
   It was idolatry no more :
      Great God they gave to Thee,

Myrrhe, frankincense, and gold ;
    But Lord, with what shall we
Present our selves before Thy majesty,
Whom Thou redeem'st when we were sold ?
W'have nothing but our selves, and scarce that
    neither,
        Vile dirt and clay :
        Yet it is soft, and may
        Impression take :
Accept it, Lord, and say, this Thou had'st rather;
Stamp it, and on this sordid metal make
    Thy holy image, and it shall out-shine
    The beauty of the golden myne.
                                Amen.


| | | |
|---|---|---|
| *A Meditation of the*<br>*Four last things* | ⎧ Death,<br>⎨ Judgment,<br>⎩ Heaven,<br> Hell | ⎫ *For the*<br>⎬ *time of*<br>⎭ *Lent e-*<br> *specially.* |

## A Meditation of Death.

DEATH, the old serpent's son,
    Thou had'st a sting once like thy
        sire,
That carried Hell, and ever-burning fire :
    But those black dayes are done ;

83

Thy foolish spite buried thy sting
In the profound and wide
Wound of our Saviour's side.
And now thou art become a tame and harmless
thing,
A thing we dare not fear
Since we hear
That our triumphant God to punish thee
For the affront thou didst Him on the tree,
Hath snatcht the keyes of Hell out of thy hand,
And made thee stand
A porter to the gate of Life, thy mortal enemic.
O Thou who art that gate, command that he
May when we die
And thither flie,
Let us into the courts of Heaven through Thee.
Allelujah.

### The Prayer.

Y soul doth pant tow'rds Thee
My God, source of eternal life :
Flesh fights with me ;
Oh end the strife
And part us, that in peace I may
Unclay

My wearied spirit, and take
My flight to Thy eternal spring ;
  Where for His sake
  Who is my King,
I may wash all my tears away
    That day.
  Thou conqueror of Death,
Glorious triumpher o're the grave,
  Whose holy breath
  Was spent to save
Lost mankinde ; make me to be stil'd,
    Thy child,
  And take me when I dye
And go unto the dust ; my soul
  Above the sky
  With saints enroll,
That in Thy arms for ever I
    May lie.

       Amen.


## Of the Day of Judgement.

GREAT Judge of all, how we vile wretches
  quake !
 Our guilty bones do ake,
Our marrow freezes, when we think

Of the consuming fire
Of Thine ire ;
And horrid phials thou shalt make
The wicked drink,
When Thou the wine press of Thy wrath shalt
tread
With feet of lead.
Sinfull rebellious clay ! what unknown place
Shall hide it from Thy face !
When Earth shall vanish from Thy sight,
The heavens that never err'd,
But observ'd
Thy laws, shal from Thy presence take their flight,
And kil'd with glory, their bright eyes, stark dead
Start from their head :
Lord, how shall we
Thy enemies, endure to see
So bright, so killing majesty ?
Mercy dear Saviour : Thy judgement-seat
We dare not, Lord, intreat ;
We are condemn'd already, there.
Mercy : vouchsafe one look
On Thy book
Of life ; Lord we can read the saving Jesus, here,
And in His name our own salvation see :
Lord set us free :

The book of sin
Is cross'd within,
Our debts are paid by Thee.
Mercy!


## Of Heaven.

BEAUTEOUS God, uncircumscribèd
 treasure
Of an eternal pleasure,
Thy throne is seated far
Above the highest star,
Where Thou prepar'st a glorious place
Within the brightness of Thy face
For every spirit
To inherit
That builds his hopes on Thy merit,
And loves Thee with a holy charity.
What ravish't heart, seraphick tongue or eyes,
Clear as the Morning's rise,
Can speak, or think, or see
That bright eternity?
Where the great King's transparent throne,
Is of an intire jaspar stone:
There the eye
O'th'chrysolite,
And a sky

87

Of diamonds, rubies, chrysoprase,
And above all, Thy holy face
Makes an eternal clarity,
When Thou thy jewels up dost binde ; that day
Remember us, we pray.
That where the beryl lies
And the crystal, 'bove the skyes,
There thou may'st appoint us place
Within the brightness of Thy face :
And our soul
In the scrowl
Of life and blissfulness enrowl,
That we may praise Thee to eternity.
Allelujah.


## Of Hell.

HORRID darkness, sad and sore,
And an eternal night,
Groanes and shrieks, and thousands more
In the want of glorious light :
Every corner hath a snake
In the accursèd lake :
Seas of fire, beds of snow
Are the best delights below,
A viper from the fire
Is his hire

That knows not moments from eternity.
Glorious God of day and night,
  Spring of eternall light.
Allelujahs, hymns and psalms
  And coronets of palms
Fill Thy temple evermore.
   O mighty God
  Let not thy bruising rod
Crush our loins with an eternal pressure :
O let Thy mercy be the measure,
For if Thou keepest wrath in store
   We all shall die,
  And none be left to glorifie
    Thy name, and tell
How Thou hast sav'd our souls from Hell.
      Mercy.

## On the Conversion of St. Paul.

FULL of wrath, his threatning breath
 Belching nought, but chains and death :
  Saul was arrested in his way
   By a voice and a light,
  That if a thousand dayes
  Should joyn rayes
  To beautifie one day,
It would not show so glorious and so bright.

On his amazèd eyes it night did fling,
That day might break within :
And by those beams of faith
Make him of a childe of wrath
Become a vessel full of glory.
Lord, curb us in our dark and sinful way,
We humbly pray,
When we down horrid precipices run
With feet that thirst to be undone,
That this may be our story.
AUelujah.


On the Purification of the blessed Virgin.

PURE and spotless was the maid
That to the Temple came,
A pair of turtle-doves she paid,
Although she brought the Lamb.
Pure and spotless though she were,
Her body chaste, and her soul faire,
She to the Temple went
To be purifi'd
And try'd,
That she was spotless and obedient ;
O make us follow so blest precedent,
And purific our souls, for we

Are cloth'd with sin and misery.
From our conception
One imperfection,
And a continued state of sin,
Hath sullied all our faculties within.
We present our souls to Thee
Full of need and misery :
And for redemption a Lamb
The purest, whitest that e're came
A sacrifice to Thee,
Even He that bled upon the Tree.


## On Good-Friday.

THE Lamb is eaten, and is yet again
Preparing to be slain ;
The cup is full and mixt,
And must be drunk :
Wormwood and gall
To this, are draughts to beguile care withall,
Yet the decree is fixt.
Doubled knees, and groans, and cries,
Prayers and sighs, and flowing eyes
Could not intreat
His sad soul, sunk

Under the heavy preasure of our sin :
　　　　The pains of Death and Hell
　　　　　　　About Him dwell.
His Father's burning wrath did make
His very heart, like melting wax, to sweat
　　　　　Rivers of blood,
　　Through the pure strainer of his skin,
　　　　His boiling body stood
　　　　　　Bubling all o're
As if the wretched whole were but one dore
　　　　To let in pain and grief,
　　　　And turn out all relief.
O Thou, Who for our sake
　　　Dids't drink up
　　　This bitter cup :
Remember us, we pray,
　　　In Thy day,
　　　When down
The strugling throats of wicked men
The dregs of Thy just fury shall be thrown.
　　　　　　　　　Oh then

Let Thy unbounded mercy think
　　　On us, for whom
　　　Thou underwent'st this heavy doom,
And give us of the well of life to drink.
　　　　　　　　　Amen.

### On the Annunciation of the Blessed Virgin.

Wingèd harbinger from bright heav'n flown
Bespeaks a lodging-room
For the mighty King of Love.
The spotless structure of a virgin womb,
O'reshadow'd with the wings of the blest Dove :
For He was travelling to Earth,
But did desire to lay
By the way
That He might shift his clothes, and be
A perfect Man as well as we.
How good a God have we! Who for our sake,
To save us from the burning lake,
Did change the order of creation :
At first He made
Man like Himself in His own Image ; now
In the more blessed reparation
The heavens bow :
Eternity took the measure of a span,
And said
Let us make our self like Man,
And not from man the woman take
But from the woman, Man.
Allelujah : we adore
His name, whose goodness hath no store.
Allelujah.

## Easter Day.

WHAT glorious light!
How bright a sun after so sad a night
Does now begin to dawn! Bless'd were
    those eyes
        That did behold
This sun when He did first unfold
His glorious beams, and now begin to rise:
It was the holy tender sex
        That saw the first ray:
Saint Peter and the other, had the reflex,
        The second glimpse o'th'day.
Innocence had the first, and he
That fled, and then did penance, next did see
        The glorious Sun of Righteousness
        In His new dress
Of triumph, immortality, and bliss.
O dearest God, preserve our souls
        In holy innocence;
        Or if we do amiss
Make us to rise again to th'life of grace
That we may live with Thee, and see Thy glorious
    face,
        The crown of holy penitence.
                Allelujah.

On the Day of Ascension.

H E is risen higher, not set :
   Indeed a cloud
  Did with His leave make bold to shroud
The Sun of Glory, from Mount Olivet.
At Pentecost He'll shew Himself again,
 When every ray shall be a tongue
To speak all comforts, and inspire
Our souls with their celestial fire ;
   That we the saints among
  May sing, and love, and reign.
        Amen.

On the Feast of Pentecost, or Whitsunday.

T ONGUES of fire from heaven descend,
  With a mighty rushing wind
   To blow it up, and make
    A living fire
Of heavenly charity, and pure desire,
Where they their residence should take :
On the Apostles sacred heads they sit,
Who now like beacons do proclaim and tell
Th'invasion of the host of Hell ;
  And give men warning to defend
Themselves from the inragèd brunt of it.

Lord, let the flames of holy charity,
    And all her gifts and graces slide
    Into our hearts, and there abide ;
That thus refinèd, we may soar above
With it unto the element of love,
    Even unto Thee, dear Spirit,
And there eternal peace and rest inherit.

                   Amen.

## Penitentiall Hymns.

### I.

LORD, I have sinn'd, and the black number
    swells
        To such a dismal sum,
That should my stony heart and eyes,
And this whole sinful trunk a flood become,
And run to tears, their drops could not suffice
        To count my score,
        Much less to pay :
But Thou, my God, hast blood in store,
And art the patron of the poore.
   Yet since the balsam of Thy blood,
   Although it can, will do no good,
Unless the wounds be cleans'd with tears before ;
Thou in Whose sweet but pensive face

Laughter could never steal a place,
Teach but my heart and eyes
To melt away,
And then one drop of balsam will suffice.

Amen.

## II.

GREAT God, and just! how canst Thou see,
Dear God, our miserie,
And not in mercy set us free?
Poor miserable man! how wert thou born,
Week as the dewy jewels of the morn,
Rapt up in tender dust,
Guarded with sins and lust,
Who like Court-flatterers waite
To serve themselves in thy unhappy fate.
Wealth is a snare, and poverty brings in
Inlets of theft, paving the way for sin :
Each perfum'd vanity doth gently breath
Sin in thy Soul, and whispers it to Death.
Our faults like ulcerated sores do go
O're the sound flesh, and do corrupt that too :
Lord, we are sick, spotted with sin :
Thick as a crusty leaper's skin ;
Like Naaman, bid us wash, yet let it be

In streams of blood that flow from Thee:
Then will we sing.
Touch'd by the heavenly Dove's bright wing,
Hallelujahs, psalms and praise
To God the Lord of night and dayes;
Ever good, and ever just,
Ever high, Who ever must
Thus be sung; is still the same;
Eternal praises crown His name.

Amen.

## A prayer for Charity.

FULL of mercy, full of love,
Look upon us from above;
Thou who taught'st the blinde man's
night
To entertain a double light,
Thine and the dayes—and that Thine too—
The lame away his crutches threw,
The parched crust of Leprosie
Return'd unto its infancy:
The dumb amazèd was to hear
His own unchain'd tongue strike his ear;
Thy powerful mercy did even chase
The devil from his usurp'd place,

Where Thou Thy self shouldst dwell, not he,
O let Thy love our pattern be ;
Let Thy mercy teach one brother
To forgive and love another,
That copying Thy mercy here,
Thy goodness may hereafter reare
Our souls unto Thy glory, when
Our dust shall cease to be with men.

## III. Job's Curse.

LET the night perish, cursèd be the morn
Wherein 'twas said there is a man-child
born !
Let not the Lord regard that day, but shroud
It's fatal glory in some sullen cloud.
May the dark shades of an eternal night
Exclude the least kind beam of dawning light ;
Let unknown babes as in the womb they lye,
If it be mention'd, give a groan and dye.
No sounds of joy therein shall charm the ear,
No sun, no moon, no twilight star appear,
But a thick vale of gloomy darkness wear.
Why did I not, when first my mother's womb
Discharg'd me thence, drop down into my tomb ?
Then had I been as quiet : and mine eyes
Had slept and seen no sorrow ; there the wise
And subtil councillor, the potentate,
Who for themselves built palaces of state,
Lie hush't in silence ; there's no midnight cry
Caus'd by oppressive tyranny

Of wicked rulers; there the weary cease
From labour, there the prisoner sleeps in peace,
The rich, the poor, the monarch, and the slave,
Rest undisturb'd, and no distinction have
Within the silent chambers of the grave.


[From "Miscellanea Sacra" (pp 11-12), as
described in Introduction, page 13 : in the Preface
(2nd edition, 1698) Tate specially refers to above :
"Some of 'em carry their sanction in the names
of their authors : such as Dr. Jeremy Taylor"..]

# NOTE.

The text in Playford's "Harmonia Sacra" presents these variations:

Line 7th, "unborn" for "unknown."

  ,, 11th, "veil" for "vale".

  ,, 19th, "oppression and the".

  ,, 20th, "here, here the weary".

  ,, 21st, "here, the pris'ner".

and at end chorus "Here, here, the weary cease". But the most extraordinary blundering of the "Harmonia Sacra" is the chaos of prose and verse at the close—repeated singularly enough by WILLMOTT in his Life of Taylor (2nd edition, 1848: p. 312) without detection or remark. As a "Curiosity of Literature" and an additional proof of how perfunctorily the Poems of our Prelate have been hitherto edited even by scholarly men, I subjoin the lines in question from WILLMOTT literally:

> " Then had I been at quiet, and mine eyes had
> slept and seen no sorrow ;
> there, there the Wise and Subtile Counsellor,
> the Potentate, who for themselves build Palaces of
>     State,
> lye hushed in Silence ; there's no Midnight cry
> caus'd by Oppression, and the Tyranny of wicked
>     Rulers.
> Here, here the Weary cease from Labour,
> here the pris'ner sleeps in Peace ;
> the Rich, the Poor, the Monarch, and the Slave,
> rest undisturbed and no distinction have,
> within the silent Chambers of the Grave.
>           *Chorus.*
>    Here, here, the weary cease, &c.  G.

# IV.

## Verse-portraits of the Four Evangelists;

FROM THE "GREAT EXEMPLAR" (1657).

---

### 1   St. Matthew.

THIS Mathew and that angel doth implie
Christe's roial ligne in His humanitie :
Mankinde Himself, deriving downe the
    same
To Joseph's tribe, from faithfull Abraham.

### 2   St. Marke.

Marke's lion—as his gospell—doth beginne
A crier's voice the wilderness within,
Make straight His pathes :  the same is onely
    Hee
Of Judah's tribe who was foretold to bee.

### 3.   St. Luke.

This holy artist with inspirèd pen
The great Messiah pourtrayes, and to men
Whose sin ore-loaded soules to death encline
Att once becomes physician and devine.[1]

---

[1] " Luke, the beloved physician "  Colossians iv. 11.  G.

4.  St. John.

Looke how the quick-sight eagle mounts on
    high
Beholds the sunne with her all-piercing eie:
So unto Christe's diuinitie I soare
Beyond the straine of those that are before.

## V.

# Aurea Catena.

## Verse Translations.

I. From "Deus Justificatus or a Vindication of the Glory of the Divine Attributes in the Question of Original Sin: in a Letter to a Person of Quality." 1656 (o12) and 1657 (folio).

### I. THE FALL.

"The main thing is this: when God was angry with Adam, the man fell from the state of grace; for God withdrew His grace, and we returned to the state of meer nature, of our prime creation. And although I am not of Petrus Diaconus, his mind, who said that when we all fell in Adam, we fell into the dirt, and not only so, but we fell also upon a heap of stones; so that we not onely were made naked, but defiled also, and broken all in pieces: yet this I believe to be certain, that we by his fall received evill enough to undoe us,

and ruine us all; but yet the evil did so descend
upon us, that we were left in powers and capaci-
ties to serve and glorifie God; God's service was
made much harder, but not impossible ; mankind
was made miserable, but not desperate; we con-
tracted an actuall mortality, but we were redeem-
able from the power of Death; sinne was easie
and ready at the door, but it was resistable ; our
Will was abused, but yet not destroyed; our
Understanding was cozened, but still capable of
the best instructions; and though the Devill had
wounded us, yet God sent His Son, Who like the
good Samaritan poured oyll and wine into our
wounds, and we were cured before we felt the
hurt, that might have ruined us upon that occa-
sion. It is sad enough, but not altogether so
intolerable and decretory [as some would make
it] which the Sibylline oracle describes to be the
effect of Adam's sin :

Ἄνθρωπον πέπλασθαι θεοῦ παλαμαῖς ἐνὶ αὐταῖς
Ὅν τε πλάνησεν ὄφις δολίως ἐπὶ μοῖραν ἀνελθεῖν
Τοῦ θανατοῦ, γνῶσίν τε λαβεῖν ἀγαθοῦ τε κακοῦ τε.

Man was the worke of God, fram'd by His hands ;
Him did the Serpent cheat, that to death's bands
He was subjected for his sin : for this was all :
He tasted good and evill by his Fall.

[Sic apud Lactant. ii. 13 : fol. Cæsenæ, 1646.
Aliter in edd-recent.]

106

AUREA GRANA.

## 2. GUILT AND DESTINY.

" To say that our actual sins should any more
proceed from Adam's fall, then Adam's fall should
should proceed from itself, is not to be imagined ;
for what made Adam sin when he fell? If a
fatal decree made him sin, then he was nothing to
blame :

> Fati ista culpa est,
> Nemo fit fato nocens.
> No guilt upon Mankinde can lie
> For what's the fault of Destiny.
> [Seneca Œdip, line 1019.]

## 3. ORIGINAL SIN.

" Because I have proved it cannot infer damna-
tion, I can safely conclude it is not formally,
properly and inherently a sin in us.
Nec placet, O superi, cum vobis vertere cuncta
Propositum, nostris erroribus addere crimen.
Nor did it please our God, when that our state
Was chang'd, to adde a crime unto our fate.
> [' Hoc placet ', &c.—Lucan vii., 58.]

## 4. NO MASTERS: ONE MASTER.

" ' They that taught of this article before me
are good guides, but no lords and masters;' for I
must acknowledge none upon Earth ; for so I am

107

commanded by my Master that is in Heaven ; and
I remember what we are taught in Palingenius,
when wee were boyes.

Quicquid Aristoteles vel quivis dicat, eorum
Dicta nihil moror a vero cum forte recedunt :
Sæpe graves magnosque famaque verendos
Errare et labi continget, plurima secum
Ingenia in tenebras consueti nominis alti
Authores, ubi connivent, deducere easdem.
If Aristotle be deceiv'd, and say that's true
What nor himself nor others ever knew,
I leave his text, and let his schollers talke
Till they be hoarse or weary in their walke :
When wise men erre, though their fame ring like
  bells,
I scape a danger when I leave their spells.

    ⌊In Poemate cui nomen ' Zodiacus vitæ ', lib.
      viii. sive ' scorpio', p. 187.—Basil 1563.
      8vo.—(It is something to know one of the
      school-books of Taylor. Barnabe Googe
      quaintly translated the ' Zodiake of Life ' :
      various editions. G.)⌋

## 5. THE SOFT ANSWER.

" If any man is of my opinion, I confesse I love
him the better, but if he refutes it, I will not love
him lesse after than I did before; but he that

dissents, and reviles me, must expect from me no
other kindness but that I forgive him, and pray
for him, and offer to reclaim him, and that I re-
solve nothing shall ever make me either hate him
or reproach him. And that still in the greatest
of his difference, I refuse not to give him the com-
munion of a brother; I believe I shall be chidden
by some or other for my easinesse and want of
fierceness, which they call zeal; but it is a fault
of my nature, a part of my original sin :

Unicuique dedit vitium natura creato,
Mi natura aliquid semper amare dedit.
Some weaknesse to each man by birth descends,
To me too great a kindnesse Nature lends.

[Propertius : lib. ii. cl. 22.17. Be it noted
that the ascription of his ' charity ' to his
original sin is a playful gibe against his
adversaries from the topic of his book;
and also, that Eden &c. misread ' refuses '
for 'refutes' in 2nd. *supra*—one of
swarming errors in the edition of the
Works current. G ]

## 6. HINDRANCES.

Qui serere ingenuum volet agrum,
Liberet arva prius fructibus,
Falce rubos filicemque resecet

Ut novâ fruge gravis Ceres eat.

He that will sow his field with hopefull seed,
Must every bramble, every thistle weed ;
And when each hindrance to the graine is gone,
A fruitfull crop shall rise of corn alone.

[al. 'liberat,' 'resecat.' Boethius, lib. iii.
metr. 1.]

## 7.  CONSCIENCE.

Extemplo quodcunque malum committitur, ipsi
Displicet authori ;—
He that is guilty of a sin
Shal rue the crime that he lies in.

[Lege ' Exemplo......malo' :  Juvenal,
Sat. xiii. I.]

## 8.  TRUE IF NEW.

" I end with the words of Lucretius,
    Desine quâpropter novitate exterritus ipsa
    Expuere eo animo rationem, sed magis acri
    Judicio perpende, et si tibi vera videtur,
    Dede manus, aut si falsa est, accingere contra.
    Fear not to own what's said because 'tis new ;
    Weigh well and wisely if the thing be true.
    Truth and not conquest is the best reward ;
        'Gainst falsehood onely stand upon thy guard.
    [Lib. ii. lines 1039 et seqq.]
        110

II. From "A Discourse of the Nature, Offices, and Measures of Friendship" 1657 and 1673 (folio) and 1678 (12o.)

## 9. FRIENDSHIPS.

" A Good man is the best friend, and therefore soonest to be chosen, longer to be retain'd; and indeed never to be parted with ; unless he cease to be that for which he was chosen :

Τῶν δ' ἄλλων ἀρετῇ ποειῶ φίλον ὅστις ἄριστοσ.*

Μήποτε τὸν κακόν ἄνἑρα φίλον ποιἑισθαι ἑταῖρον†

Where Vertue dwells there friendships make,
But evil neighbourhoods forsake.

[* Pythag. carm. aur. 5 : † Theogn. lin. 113.]

## 10. LOVE FOR LOVE.

" That was the commendation of the bravest friendship in Theocritus : "

They lov'd each other with a love
That did in all things equal prove.

. . . . . . . . . . . . . . . . ᾿Η ῥα τότ᾿ ἦσαν

χρύσειοι πάλαι ἄνἑρες ὅκ᾿ ἀντεφιλας᾿ ὁ φιλαθεὶσ·

The world was under Saturn's reign
When he that lov'd was lov'd again.

[Idyll xii. 15.]

111

## 11. MUTUAL FRIENDS.

*Ζεύς μοι τῶν τε φίλων δοίη τίσιν οἵ με φιλεῦσι·** 
*Ὄλβιοι οἱ φιλέοντες, ἐπὴν ἴσον 'ἀντεράωνται.‡*

Let God give friends to me for my reward,
Who shall my love with equal love regard ;
Happy are they, who when they give their heart
Find such as in exchange their own impart.

[* Theogn. line 337 : ‡ Bion, ap. Stob. floril,
tit. lxiii. (de Venere, &c.) 28.]

## 12.   A FRIEND NOT MONEY.

*Ἐν τοῖς δὲ δεινοῖς χρημάτων κρείττων φίλος.*

When Fortune frowns upon a man,
A friend does more than money can.

[Auct. incert. ap. Grot excerpt. ex trag. et
com. p. 945. Paris 1626. 4o.]

## 13.   A NOBLE FRIENDSHIP.

" I confess it is possible to be a friend to
one that is ignorant, and pitiable, handsome and
good for nothing, that eats well, and drinks deep ;
but he cannot be a friend to me : and I love him
with a fondness or a pity, but it cannot be a
noble friendship.

*Οὐκ ἐᾷ πότων καὶ τῆς καθ' ἡμέραν τρυφῆς*
*ζητοῦμεν ᾧ πιστεύσομεν τὰ τοῦ βίου*

112

πάτερ; οὐ περιττὸν οἷσι τ᾿ ἐξευηκέναι
αγαθὸν ἕκαστος ἐὰν ἔχῃ φίλου σκιάν·

said Menander;

By wine and mirth and every daye's delight
We choose our friends to whom we think we might
Our souls intrust; but fools are they that lend
Their bosome to the shadow of a friend.

[Line 3rd πάτερ .. υἱετ᾿, edd. recentt: ap.
Plutarch de frat. am. t vii. p. 872.]

### 14. UNSELFISHNESS IN FRIENDSHIP.

" I account that one of the greatest demonstrations of real friendship is that a friend can really endeavour to have his friend advanced in honour, in reputation, in the opinion of wit or learning, before himself:

Aurum, et opes, et rura frequens donabit amicus :
   Qui velit ingenio cedere, rarus erit.*
Sed tibi tantus inest veteris respectus amici,
   Carior ut mea sit quam tua fama tibi.†
Lands, gold, and trifles many give or lend :
But he that stoops in fame is a rare friend ;
In friendship's orbe thou art the brightest starre,
Before thy fame mine thou preferrest far.

[* Martial, lib. viii, ep. 18 : † *Ibid*, lin. 3.]

## 15.  BROTHERS.

" It is observable that ' brother ' is indeed a
word of friendship and charity and of mutual
endearment, and so is a title of the bravest society;
yet in all the Scripture there are no precepts given
of any duty and comport which brothers, that is,
the decendants of the same parents, are to have
one towards another in that capacity; and it is
not because their nearness is such that they need
none : for parents and children are neerer, and yet
need tables of duty to be described; and for
brothers, certainly they need it infinitely if there
be any peculiar duty.   Cain and Abel are the
great probation of that, and you know who said,

...... fratrum quoque gratia rara est :
It is not often you shall see
Two brothers live in amity.
[Ovid, Met. i., 145.]


## 16.  FRIENDSHIP IMMORTAL.

" We may do any thing or suffer any thing, that
is wise or necessary, or greatly beneficial to my
friend, and that in any thing in which I am perfect master of my person and fortunes.   But I
would not in bravery visit my friend when he is
sick of the plague, unless I can do him good

equall at least to my danger; but I will procure him physicians and prayers, all the assistances
that he can receive, and that he can desire, if
they be in my power: and when he is dead I will
not run into his grave and be stifled with his
earth; but I will mourn for him, and perform his
will and take care of his relatives, and doe for
him as if he were alive; and I think that is the
meaning of that hard saying of a Greek Poet,

Ἄνθρωπ' ἀλλήλοισιν ἀπόπροθεν ὦμεν ἑταῖροι·
πλὴν τούτου, πάντος χρήματός ἐστι κόρος.

To me though distant let thy friendship fly;
Though men be mortal, friendships must not die;
Of all things else ther's great satiety.

[Theogn lin. 595.]

## 17. HELP IN ADVERSITY.

" He that chooses a worthy friend that himself
in the dayes of sorrow and need might receive the
advantage, hath no excuse, no pardon, unless himself be as certain to do assistances when evil
fortune shall require them. The summe of this
answer to this enquiry I give you in a pair of
Greek verses:

Ἴσον Θεῷ σου τοὺς φίλους τιμᾶν θέλε.
ἐν τοῖς κακοῖς δὲ τοὺς φίλους εὐεργέτει·

115

Friends are to friends as lesser gods, while they
Honour and service to each other pay :
But when a dark cloud comes, grudge not to lend
Thy head, thy heart, thy fortune to thy friend.

              [Poet incert .—Grot. excerpt. p. 945.]

# Notes and Illustrations.

1. See close of Job's curse, page 46th for various readings and corrections.

2. Hymn for Advent, page 18th, line 24th. Some of the Collections if I do not err in my recollection read 'heedless': but the sequel shews that it is Christ as the Head of His body the Church that is meant. In line 11th, in 1680 (12o.) edn., a misprint 'hath' is repeated in Parker's reprint, as below.

3. *Ibid*, line 31st, 'spruce' = lively. So Milton in Comus, line 985 :

4. 2nd Hymn for Advent, page 19th, line 3rd., 'strait' = straight *i. e.* plain, ready. Cf. Isaiah xl. 3. and Mr. W. A Wright's Bible Word-Book in its place.

5. *Ibid*. Speed, as before, thus begins this Hymn,
   " Behold, we stay
   Lord, come away :
   Thy road is ready, and thy paths made strait
   With languishing expect and wait &c.

6. *Ibid*, lines 9-15 : cf St. John II. 13—17.

7. The 2nd. Christmas Hymn, page 21st, st. 3rd. lines 5—6. SPEED, as before, besides various other mis-changes, here reads,
   " The ox and mule do all behold
          With wonder,
   An homely stable should unfold
          The thunder."

117

8. *Ibid.* See Sir John Beaumont's priceless "Of the Epiphany": our edition of his Poems pp 69-70.

9. The 3rd. Christmas Hymn, page 22nd, line 12th : in 1657 edition ' sets '.

10. *Ibid,* line 13th, ' emperie ' = sovereignty or dominion In 1657 edition spelled ' empire ' which conceals the rhyme with ' free. ' Speed, as before sadly mars this Hymn.

11. The 4th Christmas Hymn, pages 22-24. As in Job's Curse from " Harmonia Sacra" and Willmott, the somewhat eccentric measure and rhythm of the opening of this Hymn are made more so by mis-printing. In the 1659 and other texts, lines 5-6 read thus :

"Goe run, and bid good-morrow to the sun,
Welcome his safe return to Capricorn".

I have had no hesitation in adopting the reading given, for which I am indebted to Dr Macdonald in " Antiphon " p 220. So in 1659, and other texts, line 14th is divided at 'mute' and thus fails to rhyme. The paradoxes of lines 19-28 recal Giles Fletcher and Herbert Palmer.

12. Lines 24th –25th : Taylor here remembered Crashaw's Hymn of the Nativity, in the full Chorus :

" Welcome all wonders in one sight !
Eternity shut in a span ".

13. Hymn on St. John's day, page 24th, line 7th : in 1657 edition the reading is ' to ' for ' by his hand '— a misprint.

14. Upon the day of the Holy Innocents, page 25th, line 13th, fontinels = little fountaines, *i e,* the breasts. So faithful Teate in his " Ter Tria ",

118

" these *fontinels* thus dri'd." (p. 107.)

15. Lines 13th and 14th : Crashaw's own rendering of
his Epigram " to the Infant Martyrs" probably
suggested this couplet. It is as follows :

" Go smiling soules, your new built cages breake,
In heaven you'l learne to sing, ere here to speake :
*Nor let the milkie fonts that bath your thirst*
          Be your delay,
The place that calls you hence, is at the worst
          *Milke all the way.*"

16. *Ibid*, line 19th : I have ventured to alter " desir'd"
into " desirèd."

17. *Ibid*. Under this Hymn cf. Nahum Tate in his
" Slaughter of the Innocents " :

" Early, but not untimely, dead :
Who to preserve the World's great Saviour bled ;

   .     .     .     .     .

If then 'tis glorious to pursue
His great example, what must be your due,
Who dy'd for Him before He dy'd for you " ?

(Misc. Sacra p 39, as before)—One does sometimes in
books as in Nature chance on a primrose glittering
with celestial dew upon a heap of sand. Earlier
than either is John Davies of Hereford—an unequal
Poet, nevertheless the undoubted possessor of *the*
true gift—in his " Muses Sacrifice," as follows :

......" to a Nation, most idolatrous.

Thou wast constrain'd, from his pursuite to flye :
So Innocence' life preservèd thus :
for which deare innocents were forc'd to dye.
Then Innocence, Innocencie slew :

119

how then could it therein be innocent ?
For both are innocent ; yet both is true ;
　　the first indeede ; the other, in event.
They lost their bloud for Him ; He His for them :
　　so both did bleede : and for each other bled :
And both as innocent, their blouds did streame,
　　He as their Head : they, members of that Head.
O had I beene so blest, ere sinne I knew,
　　t'have di'd for Thee, among those innocents :
Or, that I could my sinne, to death, pursue ;
　　or make them liue like banish'd male-contents.
Then would I dye for Thee, an innocent
　　if curst Herodian hands would blesse me so ;
O let me trie this deare experiment,
　　—although it cost my heart-bloud - ere I goe.
　　(A Meditation gratulating for our Redemption : 1612
　　　　pp 41—42.)
　　The Earl of Stirling has pathetic verses also on
　　　　" Those guiltless babes of Bethel, slain by guess."
18. Upon the Epiphany, page 26th, line 10th, misprinted
　　　" Infant's King's " and line 18th, redeem'st, is =
　　　redeemd'st.
19. Meditation of Death, pages 27-28. See Speed's version
　　　of this in our Phineas Fletcher, Vol. I. cclxxxiv-v :
　　　and context, concerning Death as degraded into a
　　　'porter', with relation to Fletcher and Milton,
　　　Davies of Hereford puts the idea in another way and
　　　very wonderfully :
　　　　How oft haue I beene at the gates of Hell
　　　　　and could not enter though I went about :

Thou did'st the diuell from his charge compell ;
so Porter wast Thy selfe to keepe me out.
"Muses Sacrifice" 1612 p 21.

20. *Ibid*, line 2nd, from end, in 1680 edition, has 'flee'
for 'flie' in error.

21. The Prayer, page 28th, line 6th, "un-clay" = dis-
embody. So Phineas Fletcher has "un-hide" (II.
289, 331 ; III. 84) and "unshade". (IV. 337.)

22. Of the day of Judgement, page 30th, line 6th
phials = vials as in Revelations xvi. 1. *et alibi.*

23. *Ibid*, line 25th, is inadvertently dropped in Parker's
reprint of the "Golden Grove".

24. On the purification of the blessed virgin, page 34th,
line 11th, on authority of 10th edition (1680) I have
dropped the superfluous 'to' before 'follow'.

25. On Good Friday, page 36th, line 34th : 1657 edition
misreads 'from' for 'for', and next line "underwent's" for "underwent'st."

26. On the Announciation..... page 37th, line 24th, "no
store" = no limitation. Cf. on "Good Friday",
line 4th from end.

27. Penitential Hymns, I, page 40th, line 10th    Dr.
Thomas Washbourne, who preceded Taylor, in his
very fine "Wounded spirit" thus sings,
" ......if that favour be too high :
Yet this I pray Thee not deny :
That soveraign balsom, though it cost Thee deer,
Thy blood I mean,
To wash me clean,
A cleansèd spirit I can bear". (our edition p 105).

28. Conversion of St. Paul, page 33rd.  Cf. here also
    Crashaw's fine Epigram on the same subject, and
    with the same antitheses.  G.


The End.

C. TIPLADY AND SON, PRINTERS, CHURCH STREET, BLACKBURN.

www.ingramcontent.com/pod-product-compliance
Lightning Source LLC
Chambersburg PA
CBHW021535270326
41930CB00008B/1266